QUANTUM COMPUTING

FOR TEENS!

Rujula Bhonde

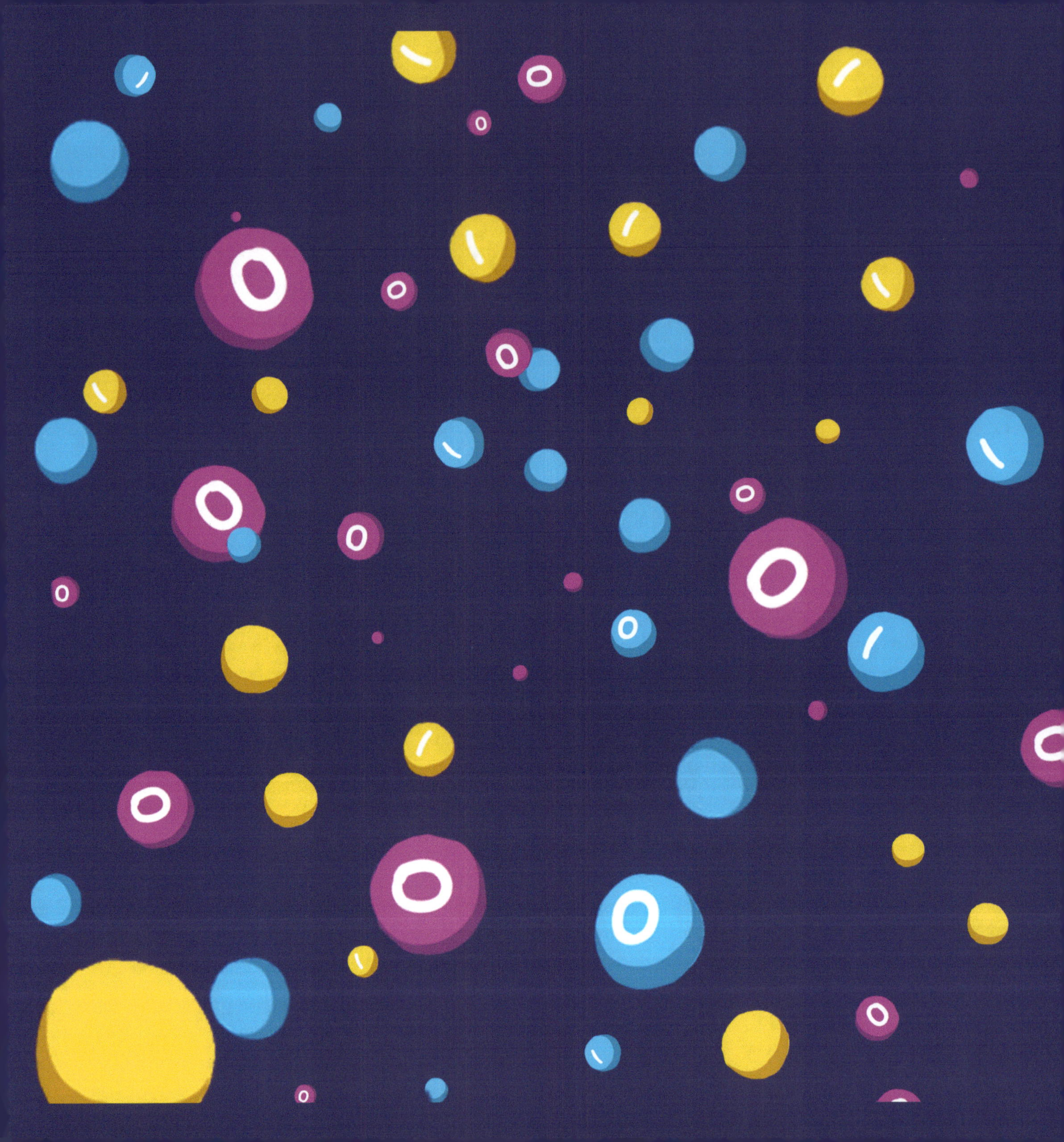

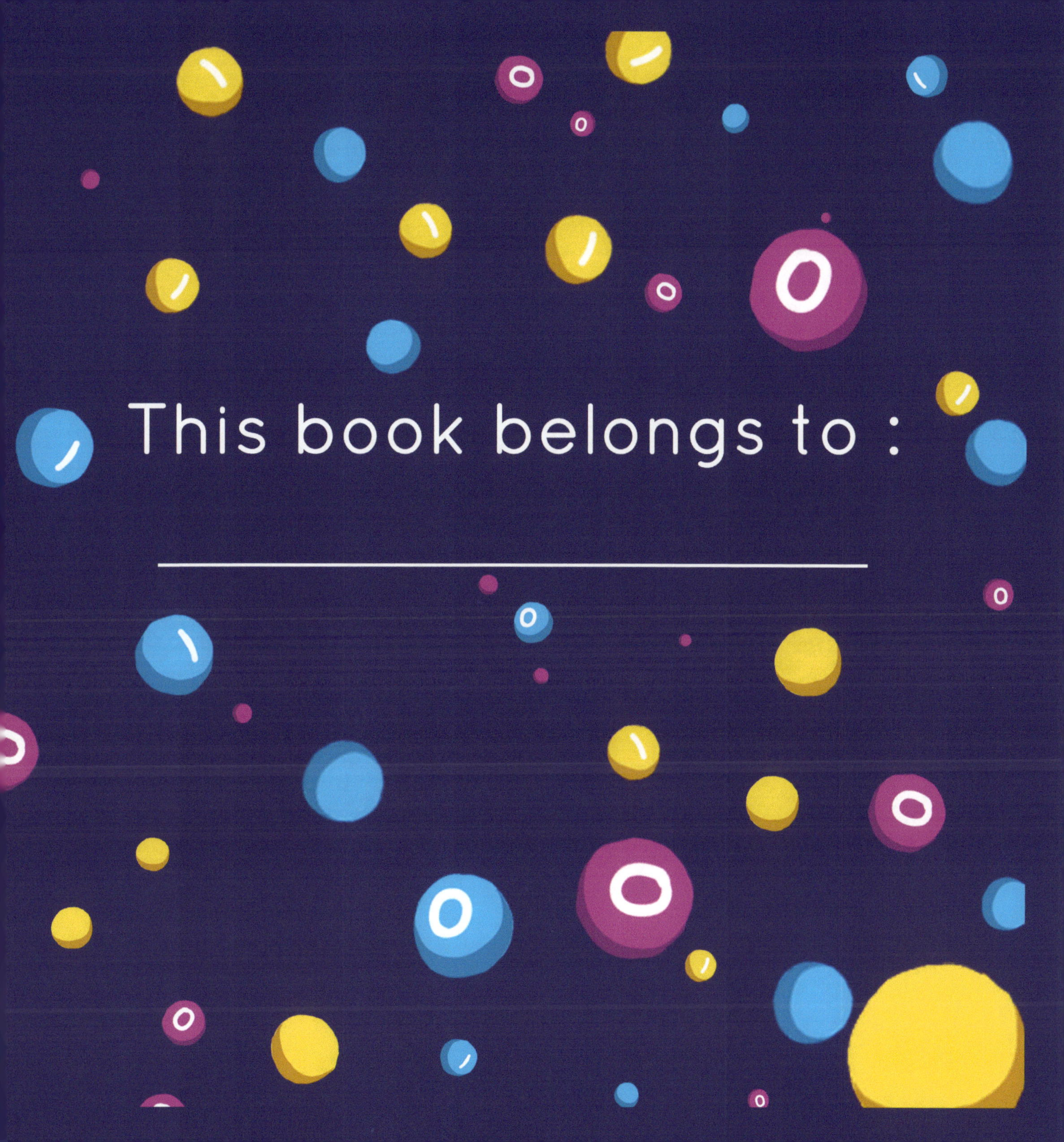
This book belongs to :

ACKNOWLEDGEMENTS

As a teen myself, the topic of Quantum Computing which was introduced to me by Makers Lab at Tech Mahindra was very intriguing. As I started trying to understand this confusing topic, the more I knew, the less I understood! It was thanks to Mr Nikhil Malhotra who explained these topics in a very simple way and inspired me to write a book for people like me.
My mother Mrs Kanchan Bhonde has been a constant support all throughout the writing, illustration, and publishing of this book. I would also like to thank my brother for sharing his computer and helping me with his jokes in stressful times. I would like to thank my entire family for their support and my teachers at ArtNotes for teaching me digital art and animation.
I would also like to thank Mr Rahul Marathe for guiding me on how a book is actually designed and his valuable reviews.
With this book, I hope that more teens like me get interested in the topic of Quantum Computing and its related fields to create a new future.

Author - Rujula Bhonde
Find me on Instagram @rujulabhonde
rujulabhonde@gmail.com

FOREWORD

Mr Nikhil Malhotra,
Chief Innovation Officer,
Tech Mahindra Ltd.

If I could somehow stop the clock today, and lie for hours in a dark open room, gazing at the stars, I would still be amazed at the expanse of the sky. It would not take me long to realize, our position in this gargantuan universe as mere mortals are nothing but a mere speck of sand, a speck that continues to flow through space and time, and be governed by discovered and undiscovered physical laws of the universe.

For ages, before Einstein , Planck, Heisenberg and Bohr, the laws laid down by Newton reigned supreme as our understanding of our universe. Not that Newton was wrong in any sense, but his laws were an approximation especially the laws on gravity. Gravity exists because a bigger more massive object pulls a smaller , lighter object towards itself and this is what we experience when we jump high, or an apple falls from the sky. It was not before circa 1915 when an idea from a young clerk in the patent office, changed our understanding on how this universe operates. Gravity does not arise because of an imaginary string between two objects, but because of the warping of space and time which is now known to be a new axis for reference as space-time.

Space and time together form a sheet of cloth spread across the universe. To draw an analogy, You can take a big sheet of cloth in your home and put a heavy globe in the center. You would notice that the piece of cloth is depressed in the center. This is exactly what heavy objects do to the fabric of space and time. Now if you take a small ball and put this from the edge of the cloth, for a small period of time, you would notice the ball moves around the big globe. That is the analogy of gravitational force. When we say the earth revolves around the sun, the earth is constantly trying to fall into the sun (it has depressed the fabric of space-time) . While it does so, the earth continues to revolve around the sun.

The aforementioned theory of relativity broke many myths, and today we consider this theory as a quintessential academic input for kids beyond a certain age. From the macroscopic objects in the classical world, the years from 1915 to today have been beautifully pockmarked about efforts to describe the very tiny or the microscopic world. This is the world where atoms, electrons and quarks live. This world is also a world which is counter intuitive and gives rise to the world that we see around us. The funny thing is that none of the features of the quantum world appear in the same way in our classical world, forcing us to think whether we live in a simulation or not.

This is what this book beautifully presents. It presents in a simple yet stunning way the laws that govern the world of subatomic particles which is also called the quantum world. The reader would find the explanation lucid and yet very interesting. You should not worry if you do not understand these concepts in the first go as that is the subtle world of quantum mechanics. It took me 3 readings to understand the superposition principle while I already was an expert in mathematics and physics.

Rujula is a teenager whose mother works at the Makers lab (R&D labs of Tech Mahindra). She came in as a young kid who could design very well but was not even remotely connected to the world of quantum physics or computing. Her trysts in the lab piqued her interest about the subject and she decided to write this book for many teens like her in the world. For her the world of quantum physics opened up a new channel to reflect her art. She studied quantum computing with me, and she tried to grasp the concepts in layman language. It is her understanding that she represented via this book.

The readers would find the explanations very intuitive and it is her and my hope that this book would take you to a path which is relatively unknown to all human kind, but a path which shows the biggest promise of change in the coming future

HAPPY READING!

CONTENTS

What do you think? I painted it myself!
Its great! But what is it?

look closely!!!
It has to be either a 6 or a 9...
Nope! Its both at the same time!!

Let me explain! Have you heard about quantum computers?
Of course not!! I don't know what quantum is, but I know what a computer is!

How's that even possible?

Computers are everywhere!

Desktops, laptops, servers, phones, TV, Fridge, Washing machine, calculators, robots, tablets, printer

Generally a computer is any object that can do addition, subtraction, multiplication, division and many other complex calculations. Today, a computer is an electronic device that can perform a series of tasks which are done according to previously set instructions. This set of instructions is called a program.
Using a program, you can do many things like storing photos, playing games, controlling a fan or washing machine and chatting with your friend. Like how we talk in many languages all around the world, computers have their own language- Binary Code using bits and bytes.

In this book, we will learn about all the things that the quantum computer can do but lets first understand what is Quantum.

WHAT IS QUANTUM?

We know that everything is made up of atoms. Grass, trees, animals, buildings etc are all made up of many different types of atoms and their mixtures (compounds). Our understanding of the world is based on this classical science.
Previously, we used to think that atoms are the smallest thing ever, but now we have discovered

smaller things which make up these atoms, called subatomic particles.
Although we cannot see them directly, we have proof that they exist.

When scientists observed these subatomic particles, they found out very unusual things. Due to their small size, the normal rules of science weren't applying to them. Quantum is a Latin word that means 'how much'. In science, Quantum physics is the study of things that are very, very small. We study the behaviour of things and the activities happening inside of atoms to make sense of the smallest things in nature.

Firstly, to understand quantum, we must know some basic terms:

1) Matter is anything that has mass
and takes up space. In other words,
it's the amount of stuff inside of an
object. So, that's why everything in
the universe is made of matter.

2) Atoms are the building blocks of
matter. The universe and everything
around us is made of atoms. Even our
bodies are made up of billions of
atoms.
Within an atom, there is a nucleus
surrounded by electrons which
circles around the nucleus.

3)Particles   -Particles are
extremely small pieces of matter, for
example, electrons, protons, neutrons

4) **Subatomic Particles** are the things that make up atoms. They can be of many different types, for example:

-**Protons** are positively charged particles that are inside the nucleus of an atom

-**Neutrons** are neutrally charged particles in the nucleus, having slightly more mass than protons

-**Electrons** are negatively charged particles which revolve around the atom.

Both electrons and protons have equal and opposite charges

Did You Know?

Electric Charge is the type of electricity present in a particle. Charge can be positive or negative.
When the positive and negative charge gets balanced, then we can say the charge is neutral

In an atom, normally the electrons and protons balance each other's charges so atoms are neutral.
When an electron is removed from an atom, it gets positively charged, and when an electron is added, it gets negatively charged

Balanced with equal number of protons and electrons

Unbalanced with more electrons than protons, becomes negatively charged

5) Wave- when you throw a stone into water, the stone disturbs the calm water and creates a ripple. This causes waves. So, a wave is a disturbance that travels through space and matter, transferring energy from one place to another. Usually, waves are repeating motions.

For example, sound waves, which are invisible, carry energy which you can hear. Different types of light waves make us see different colours of light.

Imagine yourself in the ocean or lake. Think about how far apart each wave crest is. The crest is the highest point of the wave. If you're floating on the crest of one wave and can see the crest of another, you are looking at the wavelength of that wave! The number of waves which pass through a given point in one second is called frequency of light.Imagine yourself in the ocean or lake. Think about how far apart each wave crest is. The crest is the highest point of the wave. If you're floating on the crest of one wave and can see the crest of another, you are looking at the wavelength of that wave! The number of waves which pass through a given point in one second is called frequency of light.

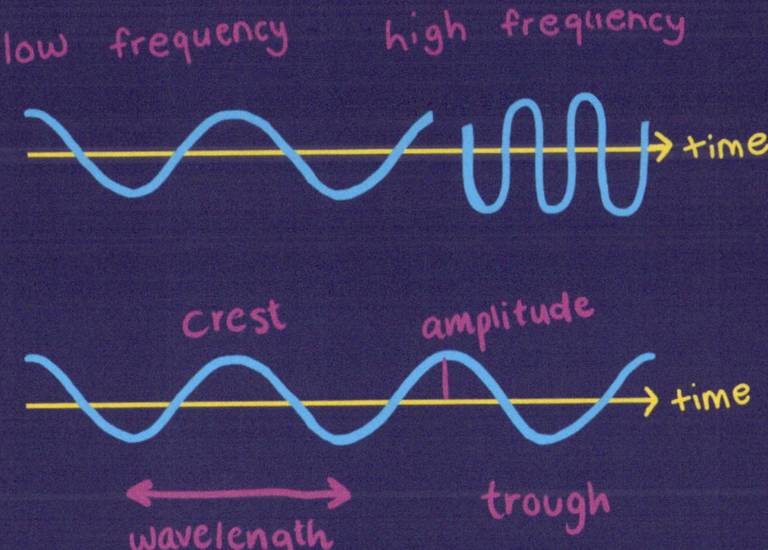

6) Photons : photons are small packets of energy that make up light.

Quantum physics is difficult to understand and has confused scientists for years. This is because humans have very little experiences with teeny tiny objects in their day-to-day lives.
These objects are always around us, but they cannot be seen without the help of powerful microscopes and other scientific instruments. This book will help you to understand how quantum physics works

and how it is used to make modern computers and solve modern problems, in a simple and fun way!

HISTORY OF QUANTUM

Lets understand a little bit about the history of Quantum Physics. This story started with Light, which is both "Weird" and "Awesome"

Light is a Wave?

In the past, Light was considered to be a wave. It was proven by the famous scientist Thomas Young with his experiment of double slits. In this experiment, he took a beam of light and shined it towards two slits, as shown below. The Light coming out of the slit was measured by a light detector. What Young observed were patterns of dark and light bands together at the back. This is called "interference".

We can see the same pattern when we throw a few stones in a still pond. The water shows waves caused by interference of multiple waves.
The banded pattern is formed when waves bumped into each other - some waves cancelled each other out causing dark bands while some added to each other causing the light bands
This experiment proved that light was a wave because it showed the wave-like patterns of "crests" and "troughs" which are like the valleys and peaks of a wave.
When two or more waves bumped into each other it caused the dark and light bands at the back of the double slits. This is why scientists thought that light was a wave.

Did you know?

Thomas Young Born in 1773 in Somerset in England, Young lived from an early age with his grandfather, eventually leaving to attend boarding school. He had loved books from the age of two, and he excelled at Latin, Greek, mathematics and natural philosophy. After leaving school, he studied medicine

He studied how vision works, discovered astigmatism and suggested that eye retina sees in three colours—something that was confirmed a century and a half later. He developed what is now known as Young temperament (a method of tuning musical instruments), the Young-Laplace and Young-Dupré equations (in fluid mechanics) and Young's rule (to calculate the infant dose of a drug). His writings for the Encyclopaedia Britannica covered 20 subjects and he even suggested a technique to improve the joints in carpentry.

In 1804 Young had become secretary to the Royal Society,. He advised on civic and national problems, such as the introduction of gas lighting to London and methods of ship construction.

Light is Interesting!

Generally the light we see is the white light which comes from the sun. But the rainbow reveals that there are multiple colours in this light.

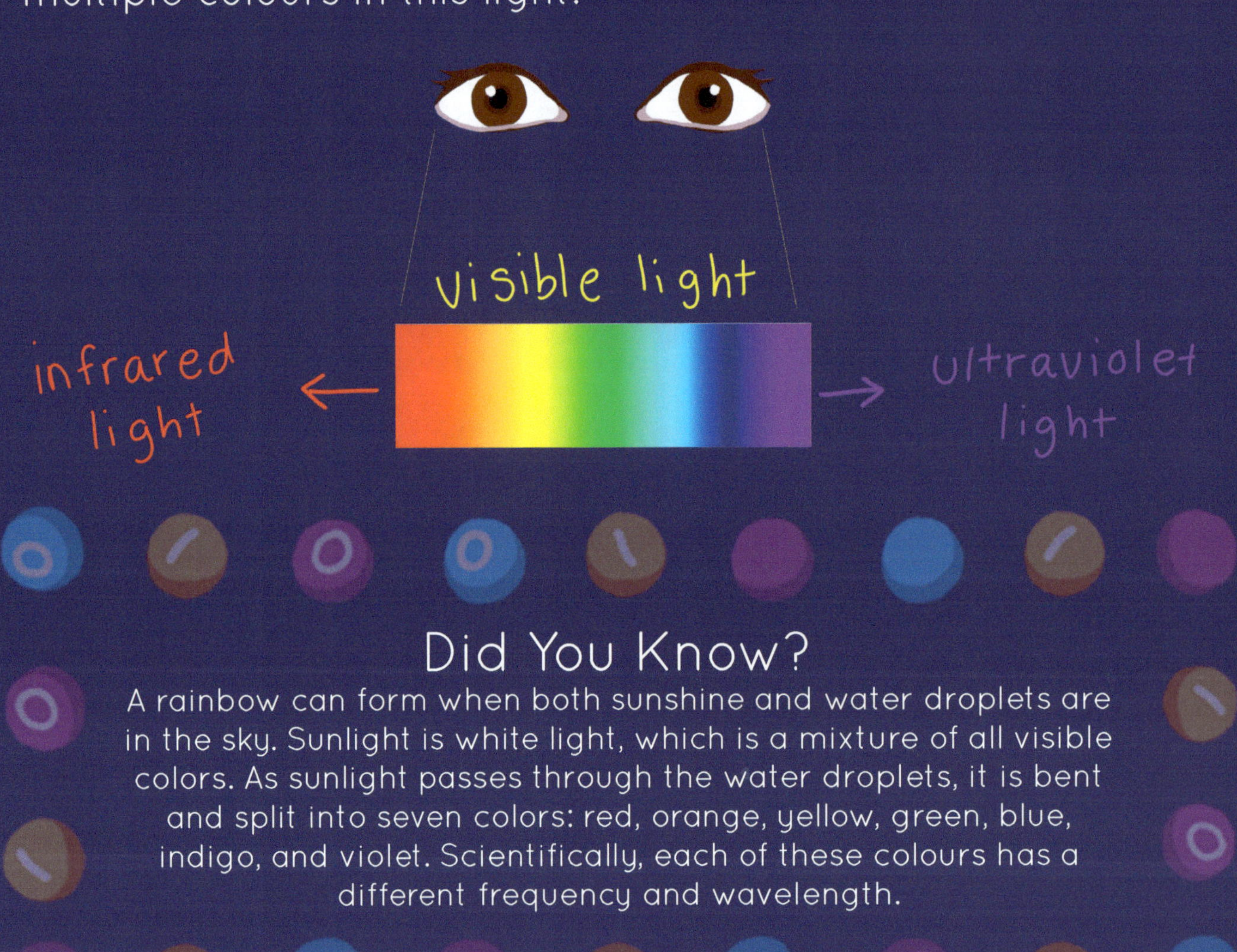

Did You Know?

A rainbow can form when both sunshine and water droplets are in the sky. Sunlight is white light, which is a mixture of all visible colors. As sunlight passes through the water droplets, it is bent and split into seven colors: red, orange, yellow, green, blue, indigo, and violet. Scientifically, each of these colours has a different frequency and wavelength.

Light is a Particle?!

Metals have a lot of loose electrons, which is why they are good conductors of electricity. In the 1900s, scientists observed that when light was shined on a metal it emitted electrons.
It was observed that only when they shined a particular coloured light on a given metal, it emitted electrons. Moreover, different metals needed different colours of light for them to emit electrons.

The scientists could not explain this phenomenon considering light as a wave, as this observation showed emission of electrons based on colours and not on the strength of light.
It was Albert Einstein in 1905 who solved this mystery by proving that light was made of separate packets of energy, called photons and these photons dispelled electrons when they had enough energy.

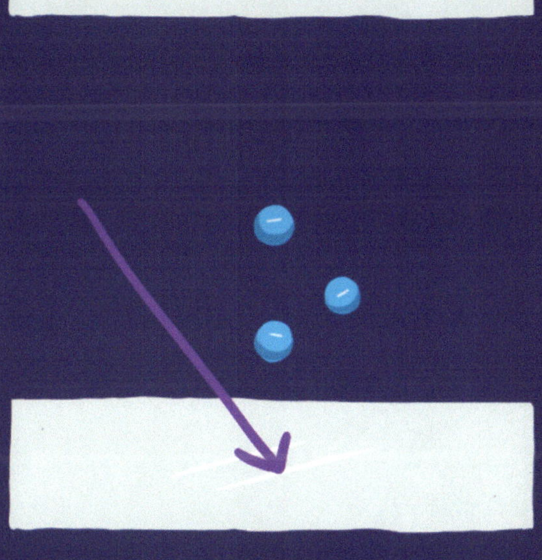

Wow! so if a wave can be a particle, can a particle be a wave?

You're right, Bit! That's exactly what Louis de Broglie thought! He suggested - "If Light is a wave that can behave as particles, can particles behave as waves?"

Did You Know

Albert Einstein was a German-born theoretical physicist who is widely held to be one of the greatest and most influential scientists of all time. His theory of relativity and became a symbol of genius that continues to inspire minds

Louie De Broglie was ridiculed by his professors. They were confused whether this guy was mad or a genius. It took none other than Einstein to realize his genius. He was indeed right. De Broglie went ahead to duplicate the double slit experiment, but this time with electrons as they are subatomic particles.

When an beam made up of particles- electrons- was shined on a double slit like in Young's experiment, the effect seen was astonishingly same as a wave. Electrons concentrated at certain positions only, just like the light wave with light and dark regions.

The dual nature of wave and particle was thus confirmed!

But how can something
be 2 things at once?!

In came another scientist named Schrodinger. He devised a thought experiment including a cat.

What did they do to the cat??

Don't worry, it was a thought experiment, no cat was harmed..

Schrodinger said, take a cat and put it in a box that is closed and has a bottle of poison in it. This poison bottle has a 50% chance of breaking which would lead to the poisonous fumes killing the cat. Is the cat dead or alive?

Well, unless the box is opened no one is sure whether the cat is dead or alive.

Inside the box, the cat is in a state of quantum randomness which can have both probabilities. Only when the box is opened and observed, the observer will know the classical state of the cat.

Did You Know?

Probability is a numerical description of how likely an event will happen. Its a value between 0 and 1. Sometimes it is also expressed as a percentage.

Looking at all these observations, the scientists came up with more theories and experimentation leading to the definition of Quantum principles. These basic principles are used to explain the phenomenon at a very small scale.

QUANTUM PRINCIPLES

There are three main principles in quantum physics:

Superposition

We have learned that light can be a wave and a particle at the same time. This is superposition. Imagine a lightbulb and its switch. In our world, it is either on or off. But in the quantum world, it can be on and off at the same

When we flip a coin, while it is in the air, it is heads and tails at the same time. Once it lands, we see that it is either heads or tails. This is superposition.

Entanglement

The famous "Jim twins," separated soon after birth in the 1940s. They lived similar lives even though they grew up far apart in completely different families. When they were reunited at the age of 39, they discovered many similarities, including the names of their sons, wives, and childhood pets, as well as their preferences for cars, carpentry etc.

A similar thing happens at a quantum level, too. The electrons, photons, and other particles that make up our universe can become linked, such that the state of one particle will be identical for the other. That connection is known as entanglement.

Little particles can push and pull on each other, and become an entangled pair, which affect each other over long distances. Even though each particle has a lot of information about the other, they do not send messages to each other, yet the particles are always connected

Tunnelling

Imagine a ball trying to roll over a hill. If the ball does not have enough energy to cross the hill, it will not be able to reach the other side. It would roll back down. In quantum mechanics, particles can, with a very small probability, tunnel to the other side, thus crossing the barrier.
The reason for this is because matter in quantum mechanics has properties of waves and particles both.

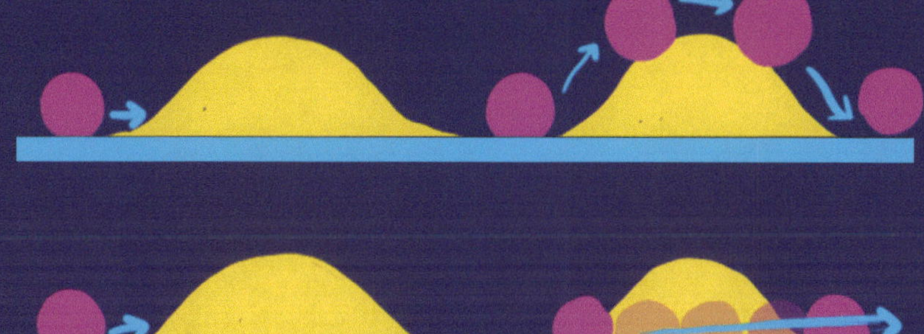

Particles like electrons cancel the effect of any thin obstacle in front of them and can travel through it, if it is thin enough.

Want to see Tunnnelling in action?
Scan this QR Code!

All these principals can be used in computers. We have made quantum computers which function in a very different way from traditional computers. Let's see how these computers work!

IBM Quantum Computer

Quantum Computing

Just as we speak in our languages, computers have their own language too. Today's computers work on the principle of Binary logic, or the language of 0 and 1. Computers are electronic circuits which contain memory and processing units. The memory stores information using numerous number of bits. These bits can have a value of either 0 or 1. The computation that happens in your computer also uses these bits.

Did You Know?

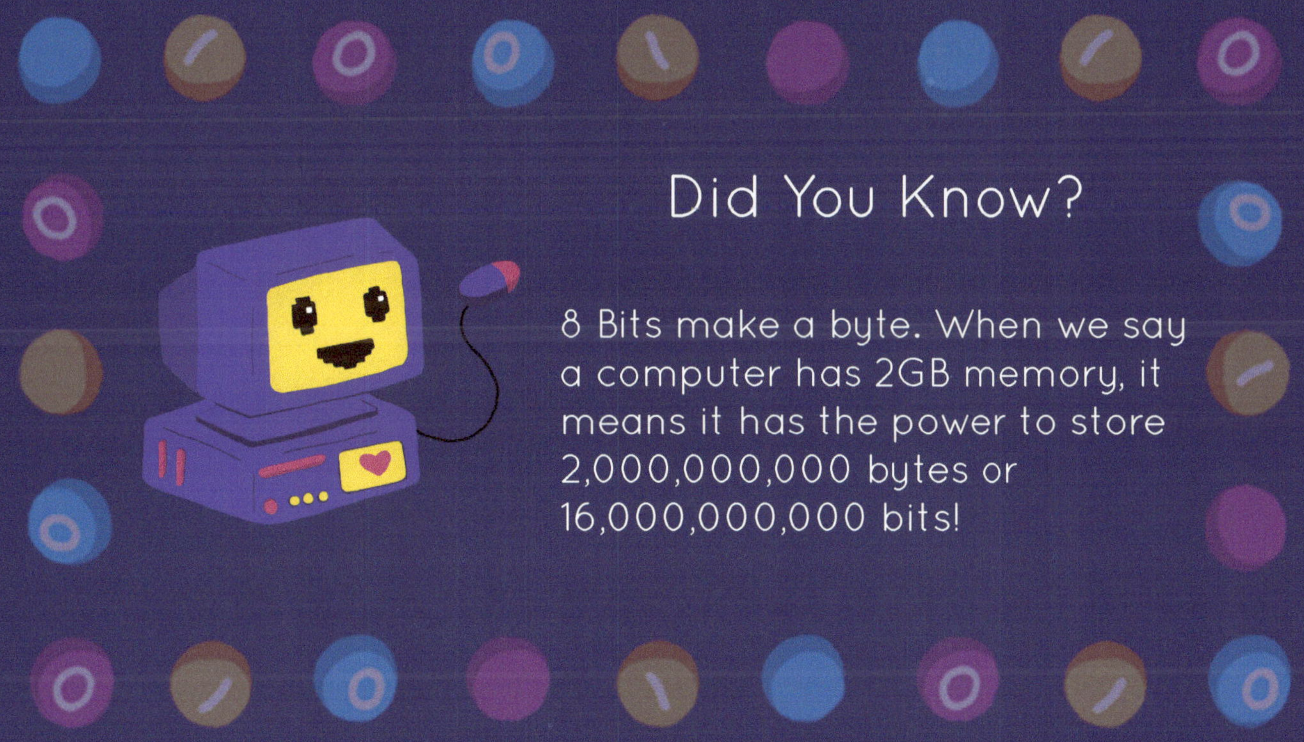

8 Bits make a byte. When we say a computer has 2GB memory, it means it has the power to store 2,000,000,000 bytes or 16,000,000,000 bits!

The Quantum world on the other hand is more probabilistic. A qubit is referred to as |0⟩ or a |1⟩, rather than just "0" or "1" . This is called a "Ket" notation.

As explained by Schrodinger's thought experiment, a Qubit can be "0" or "1" at the same time. It is only when we observe the bit can the real value be found out. So in a Quantum Computer, even with fewer Qubits, loads of computations can be done at the same time. Hence they are very fast.

So you are saying, Quantum computers can do addition, subtraction, multiplication and division – all at the same time?
But does it get all answers correct?

Yes, the Quantum computer can do that – and it can do faster than any other computer in the world!

Yes, the latest Quantum computers don't make mistakes.
Well, I don't think so. We will have the existing computers used for certain work and Quantum Computers will be used for more complex ones.

So in coming years, will the Quantum Computers replace the existing computers?

Hmm..Interesting! I have heard about massive computers which consume so much of power.

Another benefit of Quantum computers is that they consume less power so they are surely better behaved!

The main benefit of Quantum Computers is the amount of computations that can be done using this computing at the same time. A 32 Qubit Quantum computer can do parallel computations equal to the number of stars in our galaxy!

Did You Know?

To make quantum computers work, atoms must be kept stable. And the one known efficient way to keep these atoms stable is to reduce temperature to zero Kelvin($-273°$). Moreover, any kind of nearby vibration can upset the vibration of atoms which in turn creates gibberish output.

At first glance, a quantum computer resembles a giant chandelier made of copper tubes and wires — that's also what the experts call the structure, a chandelier.

Its core contains a superconducting chip on which the qubits are arranged like on a chessboard pattern.

This means the superconducting chip is located in an electromagnetic microwave field. It operates under extreme cold, at temperatures near absolute zero. For the IBM quantum computer, for example, the temperature is 0.015 Kelvin. (180 times colder than interstellar space).

Use of Quantum Computers

Quantum computers are already being used for research purposes in fields such as study of different materials, cyber security, personalized medicine, financial markets, renewable energy and more. For example, it could help to develop more efficient batteries and renewable energy sources.

Quantum computing could be used to simulate the behaviour of molecules for medicine discovery. Classical computers are limited in their ability to accurately model the behaviour of molecules, which can make this discovery a time-consuming and costly process. Quantum computing, on the other hand, can simulate the behaviour of molecules more accurately, making it possible to find medicines quickly so that in case of future pandemics or even other ailments, people don't have to wait for ages to get a new medicine!

Newer fields of study like quantum sensing and quantum communication are also developing quite well.

Classical	Quantum
Calculates with Bits which can be either 0 or 1	Calculates with Qubits which can be 0 or 1 at the same time
Consumes more power	Consumes less power
Does not have error in calculation and can be used at room tempreature	May have very small error in calculation and needs to be kept at very low temperatures
Useful for everyday processing which involves less calculations	Useful for difficult problems like Optimization, Simulations, Data Analytics

Fantastic!! This a a whole new world…. So weird and awesome!

But you did all of this to explain if the painting is a 6 or 9?! Classic Qbit!!
Of course, now you understand- it is a 6 or 9 on depending on where you see it from!!

Well, at least we learnt something about
Quantum Computing!
Did you?

EPILOGUE

Sunil Gupta
Co-Founder and CEO,
QuNu Labs

You just learnt that Quantum computing is a fascinating field which uses qubits, which can exist in multiple states simultaneously. This allows quantum computers to perform complex calculations at an exponentially faster rate than classical computers and thus has the potential to revolutionize various industries, including cryptography, drug discovery, machine learning, artificial intelligence, big data analytics, and cybersecurity.

As Nuclear Physics has vast potential for the benefit of society, but also has a negative use case of building mass destruction weapons, quantum computers in the hands of hackers can pose grave threats to data security as they can break all current key encryption algorithms. Anne Neuberger, the U.S. deputy national security advisor for cyber and emerging technology, has called Quantum Computing a "Nuclear Threat to Cybersecurity." Quantum communications deal with this threat by building encryption solutions which are safe against quantum computers.

Looking at the potential of this field, in April 2023, India announced a National Quantum Mission to develop capabilities in this field in the country. We have several start-ups working in this area in India today. It is a great time for our school and college students to explore this fascinating field and even consider a career.

I am sure while the book has initiated the readers into the world of quantum science, several questions might be cropping up in your mind and that's one of the main purposes of this exciting book

AFTERWORD

Atul Soneja
Chief Operating Officer,
Tech Mahindra Ltd.

Congratulations on completing reading the book 'Quantum Computing for Teens'! We hope you enjoyed exploring the fascinating world of quantum computing with Bit and Qubit.

Quantum computing holds a great future as it is all set to enable businesses to optimize their investment strategies, enable innovations in drug and materials discovery, financial portfolio management, climate modelling, and much more. Then again, the threat to current encryption technology by quantum is as imminent as it is real.

Huge investments and mathematical and scientific talent are currently being directed towards quantum research. Moreover, the space is ripe with competition among the private sector and start-ups. At Tech Mahindra, our Research and Innovation unit – Makers Lab is already at the forefront, dwelling on these topics and creating solutions for our clients.

While Quantum Computing is weird and awesome at the same time, it is not intuitive and is difficult to understand even for adults. Hence Rujula's attempt to simplify the topic for kids her age, with an angle of a Designer is commendable and it connects well to people of all ages.

Remember- this is just the beginning of your journey, and the real magic lies in your curiosity, creativity, and determination to continue learning. Whether you enter the field of science or not, this spirit of discovery will always be your guiding light.

I do hope that the book opens the doors for you to this astounding world of Quantum Computing. Keep asking questions, dreaming big, and never stop exploring the mysteries of the universe!

www.ingramcontent.com/pod-product-compliance
Lightning Source LLC
Chambersburg PA
CBHW041604110726
48005CB00002B/280